CRYPTOCURRENCY FOR BEGINNERS

How to Master Blockchain, Defi and start Investing in Bitcoin & Altcoins

Table of Contents

Chapter 1: Cryptocurrency Basics and Blockchain components

The term "cryptocurrency" refers to a digital currency developed via encryption techniques. Cryptocurrencies are both money and virtual accounting systems, thanks to encryption technology. You'll need a cryptocurrency wallet if you want to start using cryptocurrencies. These wallets might be software kept on your computer or mobile device, or they can be cloud-based services. Your encryption keys, which verify your identity and connect you to your bitcoin, are stored in your wallets.

Basic Knowledge to Know

It is a store of value, a medium of trade, and a unit of measurement all rolled into one. Cryptocurrencies are used to price other assets, notwithstanding their low intrinsic worth. A cryptocurrency, Bitcoin may also be seen as a speculative commodity (how much is it trading for) since it was established in 2009 and is primarily regarded as the first digital asset in existence. Blockchain and encryption have made it feasible for digital assets, often known as crypto assets, to exist. Their initial purpose was to act as a medium to transfer value without a bank or other third-party trustworthy party, and they succeeded in that goal. Digital assets (crypto assets) may be divided into cryptocurrency, commodity, and token categories. Cryptocurrencies linked to solid assets like the U.S. dollar may become an essential part of decentralized finance in the future (Defi).

To comprehend cryptocurrencies, you need also grasp the following technologies and principles:

Cryptography

Users' data and transactions are protected using cryptography, the science of scrambling and decrypting digitally signed bits of information. The term "crypto" is a euphemism for hidden or secret in the Greek language. Personal writing, or "cryptography," is the capacity to send messages that their intended recipients can only read. Cryptographic technology may provide pseudo- or true anonymity when configured correctly, depending on the settings. Encryption is used in cryptocurrency to ensure the safety of transactions and participants and the independence of operations from a central authority.

Sending encrypted communications is the most straightforward kind of cryptography, it is a method in which communication is encrypted or hidden by the sender and then decrypted by the recipient using a specified key and algorithm. In the most basic cryptography, the sender encrypts a message using a specified key and algorithm and sends the encrypted message to the receiver. Then the receiver decrypts it to decode it.

Blockchain

Bitcoin and other cryptocurrencies are built on blockchain technology. All transactions are recorded on a public ledger that is updated in real-time. The revolutionary aspect of blockchain is that it eliminates the need for a central authority, such as a bank, government, or payments business, to handle transactions. There's no need for a trusted third-party intermediary since the contracting parties interact directly. As a result, companies and services may operate independently and without expensive intermediaries.

For one thing, blockchain technology is accessible to all parties involved. Like Google Docs, the ledger may be accessed simultaneously and in real-time by various parties. When you write a check to a buddy, the cheque is deposited in the modern world, and both of you balance your checkbooks simultaneously. If your buddy forgets to update their checkbook ledger, or Things might go awry if you don't have enough cash on hand to cover the cheque. (when there is no way for the bank to foresee).

You and your partner would see the same transaction log if you use blockchain. Both of you must approve and validate the transaction before it can be put into the chain since the ledger is not under your control. Even more importantly, no one can alter the chain after the fact because of cryptography.

Distributed Ledger Technology (DLT) encompasses blockchain, a database shared by several parties (computers, servers, nodes, etc.)

Distributed Ledger Technology (DLT) This technique powers a whole coin. Accounts, balances, and transactions are all recorded in a digital ledger. Other than financial transactions, blockchain may be used to manage supply chains, monitor ownership of art, and even create digital treasures.

Node In addition to the phrase "blockchain," we'll use the term "node" throughout this essay. A node is a piece of the broader blockchain data structure. The whole system would disintegrate if there were no nodes.

Digital currencies rely on cryptography and blockchain to generate new coins, verify transactions, and build a safe system.

De-Centralized

Blockchain's decentralized means transferring power and decision-making from a centralized entity (person, organization, or group) to a distributed network. The goal of decentralized networks is to lower the degree of confidence that users must invest in one another and dissuade their capacity to assert authority or control over one another in a manner that degrades the network's performance.

All authority is shared across the network's peers, and there is no single point of failure, as shown by Bitcoin's decentralization. To "hack" Bitcoin, someone would need access to at least 51% of the machines that make up the Bitcoin network, which is regarded unfeasible.

Peer-To-Peer

Cryptocurrencies have the advantage of not requiring the involvement of a financial institution as a middleman. Because there is no "middleman," transaction costs are reduced for merchants. Customers benefit greatly if the financial system is breached or the user has faith in the conventional method. For comparison, if a bank's database were compromised or corrupted, it would be forced to recover any lost data from its backups. Even if a piece of a cryptocurrency were to be hacked, the remaining components would still verify transactional information.

There is no requirement for a third-party intermediary to facilitate cryptocurrency transfer. Users may avoid the significant transaction costs associated with conventional money transfer services thanks to minimal processing fees paid to the network. No PayPal or bank account is required.

Bitcoin Story

Investors' excitement and unhappiness with Bitcoin's potential alternatively reflect on the currency's price swings. Anonymous Bitcoin creator Satoshi Nakamoto created the currency for everyday transactions and to avoid conventional banking systems after the 2008 financial meltdown. It has since acquired popularity as a medium of exchange and attracted traders who bet against the currency's price fluctuations. As a result, it has evolved into a new investment that serves as both a store of wealth and a hedge against inflation. Even while this new story may have more validity, the past price swings were driven mainly by individual investors and traders wagering against a rising price without many bases in reason or facts.

In recent years, though, Bitcoin's pricing narrative has evolved. The cryptocurrency markets are maturing, and regulatory bodies are developing regulations expressly for institutional investors. Even though the price of Bitcoin is still fluctuating, it is no longer a tool for speculators seeking quick riches.

The following is a brief history of Bitcoin:

2009 TO 2015

At its inception in 2009, Bitcoin had no value. This product's price went to $.09 on July 17, 2010. From $1 on April 13, 2011, to a high of $29.60 on June 7, 2021, Bitcoin's price increased by 2,960 percent in three months. Bitcoin's price fell to a low of $2.05 in mid-November after a substantial decline in cryptocurrency markets. The next year, it rose from $4.85 on May 9 to $13.50 on August 15 of the same year. For Bitcoin, 2012 was a relatively quiet year, but 2013 witnessed a significant increase in the currency's value. In January, it was trading at $13.28; on April 8th, it was trading at $230; on July 4th, it was trading at $68.50. It was selling at $123.00 in October, and by December, it had soared to $1,237.55 before falling to $687.02 three days later. The value of Bitcoin fell to $315.21 by the end of 2014.

2016 To 2020

Coins like Ethereum and Litecoin have emerged to challenge Bitcoin's dominance in the digital currency market. Over the year, prices gradually increased to over $900. At the beginning of the year, the cost of Bitcoin was approximately $1,000, but it rose to almost $19,000 on December 15 after breaking the $2,000 barrier. For the following two years, Bitcoin's price hovered in a narrow range with occasional spurts of activity. As an example, in June 2019, the cost of bitcoin surpassed $10,000, and the volume of trade surged. By the middle of December, it had dropped to $6,635.84. When the COIVD-19 epidemic struck in 2020, Bitcoin's price surged to new heights. Bitcoin was valued at $6,965.72 at the beginning of the year. Government policies during the epidemic closure added fuel to investors' anxieties about the global economy, which in turn fueled the ascent of Bitcoin. On November 23, the price of one bitcoin was $19,157.16. By the end of 2020, the cost of one bitcoin had risen by 416 percent, too little under $29,000.

2021-Present

By January 7, 2021, the bitcoin price had risen over $40,000, shattering the previous record set in the year 2020. A new all-time high in Bitcoin value of almost $60,000 was reached when cryptocurrency exchange Coinbase went public in mid-April. Thanks to this increased demand, institutional buying pushed Bitcoin's price to $63,000 on April 12, 2021. By the summer of 2021, prices had fallen by half to $29,795.55 on July 19. In September, prices hit $52,693.32 before plunging to $40,709.59 after a significant drop. On November 7, 2021, Bitcoin reached a new record high, reaching $67,549.14. In early December 2021, Bitcoin was trading at $49,243.39.

Decentralized Finance

Using distributed ledgers like those used by cryptocurrencies, Defi is an emerging financial technology. Banking and financial institutions are no longer in charge of the money, economic goods, and services.

Defi has several appealing features for users, including:

- Banks and other financial institutions no longer charge fees for utilizing their services.
- Instead of putting your money in a bank, you use a safe digital wallet.
- Anyone with an internet connection may use it without getting permission from a manager.
- In a matter of seconds or minutes, you can move money throughout the world.

Understanding Defi

Understanding how centralized finance differs from Defi is essential to comprehend how Defi operates.

Centralized Finance

Banks, for-profit businesses whose only purpose is to earn money, hold your cash under centralized finance. Several third parties enable money transfers between parties, each collecting a charge in the financial system. Suppose, for example, that you use your credit card to buy a gallon of milk. Credit card networks get the information from the acquiring bank, passing it to the merchant.

The network contacts your bank to collect payment for the cleared charge. After the acquiring bank has approved the bill, the network transmits the approval back to the merchant. For the most part, retailers must pay for the privilege of using your credit and debit cards. In addition to the high cost of other financial activities, loan applications might take days to be accepted, and you may not be allowed to utilize a bank's services while abroad.

Decentralized Finance(Defi)

Financial transactions may now be carried out directly between individuals, corporations, and merchants using new technologies. To do this, peer-to-peer networks require security protocols, connection, software, and hardware developments to make this possible. Using software that records and validates financial transactions in distributed financial databases, you may lend, trade, and borrow from wherever you have an internet connection. In a distributed database, all users may access the same information, and the database utilizes a consensus technique to verify that the data is correct.

Decentralized finance leverages modern technology to abolish centralized finance models by making financial services available to anybody, independent of their identity or location. Personal wallets and trade services tailored to the needs of people are available via Defi apps, giving consumers more control over their money. However, decentralized finance does not guarantee anonymity, even while taking external parties' authority away. The organizations that have access to your data can track your transactions even if you don't. This might be a government agency, a law enforcement agency, or any other entity that exists to defend the financial interests of individuals.

- Financial transactions may now be completed without the involvement of third parties, thanks to Defi, a kind of decentralized finance.
- Defi is made up of stable coins, software, and hardware that can build apps.

- Regulation and infrastructure for Defi are currently being developed and debated.
- Two of Devi's primary objectives are reducing transaction times and making financial services more widely available.

Working Of DeFi

The blockchain technology that cryptocurrencies use is used in decentralized finance. A distributed and secure database or ledger is known as a blockchain. Decentralized applications, or dApps, power the blockchain. Transactions are recorded in blocks on the blockchain and then cross-verified by other people. In this case, the block is closed and encrypted; a new block that contains information about the preceding one is produced. The word "blockchain" refers to the fact that each block is linked to the previous one by the information contained in the preceding one. There is no method to edit a blockchain since information in prior blocks cannot be modified without impacting the succeeding ones. A blockchain is safe because of these and other security mechanisms.

Defi Crypto Trading

Another use of decentralized finance is the use of decentralized exchanges. Digital currencies are often held and moved through a system of titles or ownership via regular exchanges. Coins are not stored in a central location or function in a decentralized exchange. The exchange or organization enables, safeguards, and secures a peer-to-peer operation. Binance operates as a controlled exchange. The cryptocurrencies that are traded on Binance are held in a single location.

Founded by the Binance organization, Binance Dex is a decentralized exchange. The buyer and seller negotiate the transfer of cryptocurrency shares from one account to another. Binance Dex facilitates transactions and often charges a transaction fee for buyers and sellers.

One of Koinal's primary partners is Binance, a prominent cryptocurrency exchange that sells Defi goods (Binance Dex). You may use decentralized exchanges like Binance Dex and Koinal to buy cryptocurrencies that you can then trade or sell as you see fit.

Defi Financial Products

Defi is based on the idea of peer-to-peer (P2P) financial transactions. Two parties agree to trade cryptocurrencies for products or services, and a third party is engaged in a P2P Defi transaction. Consider the process of applying for a loan in centralized finance to grasp this properly. To get one, you'd need to apply at your bank or another lending institution. To use the lender's services, you'd have to pay interest and service fees if you were approved.

There are several ways to make a payment on your dApp, and they all go through a similar sequence of events. Using a dApp, you would submit your loan requirements, and an algorithm would match you up with other borrowers that fit your criteria. To get your money, you'd have to agree to one of the lender's conditions. It is recorded on the blockchain, and you will get your loan when the consensus process validates it. Finally, you may start making the agreed-upon repayments to your loan provider.

DeFi Currency

For transactions, DeFi is meant to work with bitcoin. It is impossible to predict how current cryptocurrencies will be applied, if at all, since technology is continuously evolving. A stable coin, a cryptocurrency backed by an institution or tied to a fiat currency like the dollar, is a crucial part of the idea.

The Future of Defi

The field of decentralized finance is still in its infancy. There are many infrastructure errors, hacks, and frauds to contend with in the uncontrolled cryptocurrency environment.

As a result of distinct financial jurisdictions, the regulations that now govern the financial industry were developed. The potential of Defi to conduct borderless transactions raises important issues for this form of code. For example, who is responsible for investigating a financial crime across international boundaries, protocols, and Defi apps?

Existing financial regulations may potentially be challenged by the open and dispersed character of the decentralized finance ecosystem. System stability, energy consumption, and carbon imprint are other issues to consider.

Before Defi can be safely used, there are still a lot of unanswered concerns and breakthroughs to be made. If Defi works, it's more than probable that banks and companies will find methods to get into the system; if not to control how you access your money, then at least to earn money from the system. Financial institutions will not give up one of their key sources of generating money.

Chapter 2: Basic Trading Strategies

Other asset classes haven't been able to keep up with the advances. One technique for investing in Bitcoin is to purchase and hold. Holding cryptocurrencies like bitcoin has been a beneficial long-term strategy. This is particularly true during crypto bull markets when corrections tend to be brief. However, investors must keep in mind that Bitcoin and other cryptocurrencies are very speculative investments and should be treated.

The previous performance of an investment does not guarantee future success. There is a slew of options available to those who want to try their hand at day trading. Technical analysis may be one of the most popular trading tactics since it has spawned whole communities of traders. Short-term traders must have a trading strategy based on rules to succeed. The following are five methods for trading cryptocurrencies throughout the day.

Technical Analysis

Technical analysis (TA) uses mathematical indicators and chart patterns to anticipate the direction of prices. Humans are required to identify specific technical indicators, such as the RSI. In contrast, others may be created by a computer tool like Trading View (For example, the cup-and-handle design).

The relative strength index (RSI) is a well-liked technical indicator (RSI). Charts with a value between 0 and 100 will show this as a single line. The more the RSI approaches 100, the more overbought the market is considered to be, indicating that prices may fall. As the RSI approaches zero, oversold circumstances are believed to exist, which might lead to a surge in prices. When it comes to day-trading cryptocurrencies, TA may be a helpful tool.

Sentiment Analysis and the News

The cryptocurrency market may be moved swiftly by significant news events on occasion. Short-term traders may not utilize headlines and general market mood, but it may still be employed in day-trading Bitcoin. When this article was first published in mid-April 2021, Turkey declared that it would no longer accept Bitcoin and other cryptocurrencies as payment alternatives inside its borders.

An immediate 3.2 percent drop in Bitcoin's value was followed by more than a 10 percent drop afterward. The mood of the most popular cryptocurrencies may also be tracked by examining Twitter activity. According to this idea, more optimistic emotion is generated by tweets praising a cryptocurrency, whereas more bearish sentiment is generated by tweets criticizing it.

Speculative Trading

Assuming prices tend to stay inside a particular range, range trading works. A support or a resistance level may be used as a trigger for traders to purchase or sell. Candlestick charts with support and resistance levels are used in this method.

Or, if prices reach a point of resistance, they may decide to go short and then cover their short when prices return to a topic of support. In the context of range-bound trading, pivot points serve as an illustration. Calculating pivot points offer investors a sense of where price reversals are likely to occur.

Scalping

This method aims to make money from modest price changes over short time frames. Market inefficiencies like bid-ask spread or liquidity gaps are often to blame. To increase their profits, "scalpers" often employ leverage, such as margin or futures contracts, to profit from even the most minor price changes.

Scalping is best suited to experienced traders because of its fast-paced and high-risk nature. However, this also increases the likelihood of losses, making risk management more critical when using this technique. Scalpers may use a variety of technical indicators, such as volume heatmaps or order book analysis to discover the best times to enter and exit trades.

Bot Trading

Using bots or high-frequency trading (HFT) is a way to execute many deals using algorithms and trading bots swiftly. A solid grasp of complex trading methods and programming is required for this approach. High-frequency traders don't just sit back and let a computer program handle their cryptocurrency trading. Developing a trading strategy, creating a program to carry out that plan, and monitoring, backtesting, and upgrading the algorithms are all part of the process of building a trading bot.

Trading bots that have already been made and are ready to use may be purchased from specific merchants. Why aren't people utilizing the bot since it's lucrative and straightforward to use? If so, why aren't its developers doing so instead of using it themselves?

Long Position

When investors take a long (buy) position, they hope the price will go up. A rising cost is a good news for a long-term investor. Long stock asset purchases are the norm when it comes to stock purchases. An investor who acquires a call option has a long call position. Consequently, an increase in the underlying asset price favors a long call. The purchase of a put option is required for a long-put position. Puts and long calls both use the same rationale to justify their "long" aspects when the value of the underlying asset decreases, the value of a put option increases — the value of a long-put increase as the value of the underlying asset decreases.

- In a long-term asset transaction, the risk of losing money is limited to the purchase cost. Benefits are almost limitless.
- The dangers of holding long calls and puts are more nuanced. In our choices case study, we examine these issues in further detail.

Investments made to see its value grow are known as long positions (also known as long positions). The term "long position" is most often associated with derivatives and forex, although it may be used for just about any asset or market. It is possible to buy a purchase on the spot market to hold it for an extended period. It is the most typical investment method, particularly for just beginning individuals. It is assumed that the asset would rise in value in long-term trading methods like purchase and hold.

To put it another way, purchase and hold is just a long-term strategy. On the other hand, you are long doing not always imply that the trader intends to profit from a price increase. Take, for example, tokens that can be leveraged. Inversely connected to Bitcoin's price is BTCDOWN. When Bitcoin's value rises, so does the value of BTCDOWN. Whenever the price of Bitcoin drops, the cost of BTCDOWN increases as well. A decline in the price of Bitcoin is exactly what you'd expect if you had a long position on BTCDOWN.

When should a long position be taken?

Depending on the period you're working with, you could be interested in going long when the price of a cryptocurrency seems like it's set to move up. For example, on the daily chart, if you anticipate the price will rise in the days or weeks to come, you may go long.

The asset may be purchased on a spot market, or a long position can be opened via futures, options, or other derivatives contracts. Your selection must, of course, be supported by some fundamental or technical analysis. High-profile cooperation or a significant improvement to the platform may prompt you to consider going long on the native token of the blockchain project.

To get a clear picture of the market mood, it's a good idea to be active on social media and keep up with current events. An alternative or additional method is looking for patterns on the charts, such as whether or not the price has broken over a key resistance line, which might imply the continuation of an upward trend.

If you aim to go long, you should be sure that the price will rise no matter what form of research you use. If you don't, you'll be going against the grain of the market. Like corporate shares, cryptocurrencies are traded against fiat currencies, such as the US dollar, constantly aiming to raise. This is unlike foreign exchange pairings, which have no long-term goal. As a result, when it comes to Bitcoin, you'll see many investors opt for the "buy and hold" approach.

Short Position

The opposite of a long position is a short position. The investor and advantageous to him desire a decrease in the security's price. Executing or initiating a temporary position is more complicated than acquiring an asset. An investor with a temporary stock position expects to make money if the stock's price falls. When a stockbroker lends you a certain number of shares, you sell them at the current market price. There will be an open position in the investor's account that must be closed at some point in the future. If the price declines, the investor may buy X number of stock shares at a lower price than they paid for the same number of shares before. The extra money is theirs to keep. Many investors find it challenging to comprehend the notion of short selling, yet the method itself is relatively easy. Let's have a look at an example to see if it helps. Stock "A" presently trades at $50 per share. If you believe that the stock price will decrease shortly, you may benefit by selling short. The following is how a short sale might go:

Optimal time to enter a short position for traders?

If you think the price of a specific cryptocurrency will fall for some time, you may want to consider selling short. As previously said, you should rely on market research to support your conclusion. In general, short-sellers initiate positions when the market has reached an overbought level—i.e., the uptrend may have been oversaturated—and the demand has been rising for a lengthy duration. Going short is also an option when the price fails to break a resistance level and begins to deviate from it. It might be challenging to analyze Bitcoin (BTC) and altcoins since the market is still in its infancy, and there aren't any solid fundamentals to support the changes. Before making a long or short trade, you should, of course, consider all of the market's influences.

- To get a loan of 100 shares of stock from your brokerage business, you put up a margin deposit in the form of collateral.
- After receiving your broker's loan of 100 shares, you immediately sell them for $50 each. Your 100 shares are gone, but you've got $5,000 in your bank account thanks to the buyer ($50 multiplied by 100 equals $5,000). It is claimed that you are "short" the stock if you owe 100 shares to your broker. (Imagine if you told someone, "I'm short 100 shares of what I owe my broker.")
- The stock's price has started to plummet, as expected. After a few weeks, the stock price has fallen to $30 a share. You decide to complete the short sale because you don't think it will drop further.
- You now pay $3,000 for 100 shares of the stock ($30 x 100 = $3,000). To repay your broker for the 100 shares he gave you, you hand over those 100 shares of stock. By returning the 100 shares borrowed, you've ended your position as a "short" on the stock.
- Your short sell transaction brought in a profit of $2,000 for you. After selling 100 shares, your broker borrowed you for $5,000 and then purchasing 100 shares to repay him for just $3,000, you got $5,000. Figure your profit this way: Received $5,000 - $3,000 = $2,000 paid (profit).

Short stock positions are usually only provided to accredited investors because of the high confidence level required between investor and broker. It is common for investors to be asked to put up a margin deposit or other kind of collateral with their broker even if their short position is successful.

HODL Crypto

In the Bitcoin investing community, the phrase "HODL" is often heard. You may use it as an investing technique and a term of art. "Hold" is a "hold" type with an intriguing backstory. In addition, the word extended to other cryptocurrency groups.

- "HODL" is a type of "hold," referring to cryptocurrency investors' buy-and-hold strategy.
- Holding lets investors avoid short-term losses from cryptocurrency volatility and benefit from long-term value increases via the "holding" technique.
- While "holding" is less dangerous in theory than trading, investors must still consider the risk of changing regulations and the general public's viewpoint.

Cryptocurrency "HODLing"

Blockchain technology underpins cryptocurrency, a kind of digital cash. There are several uses for this currency, including trading, investing, and even as a means of exchange. Coins like Bitcoin, Litecoin, Ethereum, and Ripple are all examples of cryptocurrencies. Because a central bank does not issue bitcoin, it has a significant characteristic and advantage: decentralization. The great breakouts in 2017 and 2020 have led to a surge in interest in cryptocurrencies as an investment option. Digital currencies have the opportunity to expand as the trend toward financial decentralization and decentralization continues.

Investors are also holding cryptocurrencies as a value reserve in the post-COVID low-interest climate. It is a term used to describe the buy-and-hold investment approach. Long-term value appreciation is a primary motivation for buy-and-hold investors, who often hang on to their investments for at least five years.

On the other hand, traders are considerably more active in their transactions and look for profits by buying cheap and selling high. Traders may take advantage of the extreme volatility of cryptocurrencies by taking long and short bets, which can be liquidated at will. On the other hand, holding may provide more security to investors since it shields them from short-term volatility and the danger of overpaying for a stock.

"HODL 's" History

An investor's remark on the Bitcoin Forum, where they may voice their thoughts on Bitcoin and the economy, gave rise to the term "HODL." As "HOLDING" is the misspelling of "HOLDING," a forum user with the pseudonym "Game Kyuubi" created an article titled "I am hoarding!" in December 18, 2013. That the post's author made, the right choice has been shown. Bitcoin had a banner year in 2013. The price went from $15 in January to almost $1,100 at the beginning of December, which resulted in a 7,230 percent return. The price decreased from $716 to $438, a 39 percent drop. Possibly due to China's central bank's restriction on third-party payment businesses operating with Bitcoin exchanges, the price of Bitcoin fell. As opposed to engaging in more frequent trading, many who invest in cryptocurrencies do so over the long term, a strategy known as "buy-and-hold" investing. Midway through 2017, the price of Bitcoin launched a new boom that culminated in a record high of $19,167 for the year. A year later, in early 2021, it set a new all-time high of well over $58,000 after the COVID-19 pandemic.

Chapter 3: How to buy a Crypto

<u>Choose a Cryptocurrency Broker or Cryptocurrency Exchange</u>

Before you can acquire cryptocurrencies, you'll need to find a broker or exchange. Both allow you to develop cryptocurrency, but there are a few essential distinctions to bear in mind.

Cryptocurrency Exchange

To trade cryptocurrencies, buyers and sellers must cooperate on a cryptocurrency exchange. For beginner crypto investors, deals might be scary because of their more complicated interfaces, including several trading kinds and detailed performance charts. Coinbase, Gemini, and Binance are a few well crypto exchanges. The US. Even though the standard trading interfaces of these organizations might be intimidating to novice investors, they also provide user-friendly and simple buying choices.

The Flexibility of use comes down to the fact: beginner-friendly choices charge much more than each platform's conventional trading interface to acquire the same coin. Before making your first crypto buy, or not long after, you may want to learn enough to use the traditional trading platforms to save money.

As a beginner to crypto, verify that the exchange or brokerage of your choice allows US dollar transfers and purchases. Many cryptocurrency exchanges can't buy cryptocurrency directly with another cryptocurrency; As a result, you'll have to go via a different exchange to get the tokens you need.

Cryptocurrency Broker

By communicating with exchanges on your behalf and providing clear user interfaces, brokers make the process of purchasing cryptocurrencies easier. Some levy costs are much greater than the fees charged by exchanges. Many "free" brokers make money by selling information about your transactions to major brokerages or funds or by not carrying out your business at the best available market pricing, both of which are deceptive trade practices. Two of the best-known cryptocurrency brokers are Robinhood and SoFi.

Digital wallets may not seem like a huge problem, but advanced crypto investors prefer to keep their currencies in them. Even though brokers are undeniably convenient, You need to be informed that transferring your bitcoin off the site may be difficult. You cannot withdraw any of your crypto assets while utilizing Robinhood or SoFi, for example. Some cryptocurrency users opt for offline, non-internet-connected hardware wallets for an extra layer of protection.

Create an account and verify it

Preventing fraud and complying with federal regulations necessitates taking this step. Signing up for an account with a cryptocurrency broker or exchange is easy after you've decided on one. You may have to prove your identification depending on the platform and the amount you want to purchase. When the verification procedure is complete, you may not be able to do so to buy or sell any cryptocurrency. Even a selfie may be required to verify that the papers you provide match your look on the site, which may need your driver's license or passport.

Make a cash deposit to invest.

You'll need to have money in your account before purchasing cryptocurrency. If you're using a debit or credit card, you may make a payment by connecting your account to your crypto wallet and requesting a wire transfer. You may have to wait a few days to use the money you deposit for certain exchanges and brokers to buy cryptocurrencies. One word of caution before you buy: While you may deposit money with a credit card at certain exchanges or brokers, doing so is exceedingly risky — and costly. As cash advances, credit card issuers accept cryptocurrency transactions made with a credit card. As a result, you'll pay more excellent interest rates and extra cash advance costs than you would on everyday purchases. When you take out a cash advance, you may be charged a fee of 5% of the transaction amount. Assuming that your crypto exchange or brokerage charges costs of up to 5 percent, this means you might lose 10% of your crypto buy to fees.

Submit a Cryptocurrency Order

A bitcoin order may be placed as soon as the funds in your account are available. Cryptocurrencies like Bitcoin and Ethereum are well-known, but there are other less prominent coins like Theta Fuel and Holo.

You may enter the ticker symbol (Bitcoin is BTC, for example) and the number of coins you wish to purchase when picking which cryptocurrency to buy. A fractional share of high-priced tokens like Bitcoin or Ethereum may be bought on most cryptocurrency exchanges and brokers.

Cryptocurrencies with the highest market capitalization are listed below:

- The cryptocurrency is known as Bitcoin (BTC)
- The Ethereum virtual currency (ETH)
- Tethered (USDT)
- Bitcoin (BNB) (BNB)
- The city of Cardano (ADA)
- The Dogecoin cryptocurrency (DOGE)
- A cryptocurrency denoted by the symbol XRP (XRP)
- The currency of the United States (USDC)
- A polka-dot background (DOT)
- Uniswapping (UNI)

Choose a Storage Method

Money worth millions of dollars in Bitcoin is already gone because people forgot or lost the codes to their accounts. As a result, cryptocurrency exchanges are vulnerable to hacking and theft since they are not insured by the Federal Deposit Insurance Corporation (FDIC). That's why having a safe location to store your cryptocurrency is so crucial.
To reiterate, you may have little to no control over how your bitcoin is held if you acquire it via a broker. More possibilities are available if you buy cryptocurrencies on an exchange.

The crypto should remain in the exchange

As soon as you purchase a cryptocurrency, it is generally kept on the exchange in a "crypto wallet." A hot or cold wallet is a good alternative. If you don't trust the service, your exchange utilizes or wants to keep it out of the public eye. A minor charge may be required depending on the exchange and the amount of money you are transferring.

Hot wallets

These are online crypto wallets that can be accessed from any internet-enabled device, including smartphones, tablets, and laptops because they're still linked to the internet and pose a more significant theft risk.

Cold wallets

Because they are not linked to the internet, cold crypto wallets are the safest way to store your bitcoin. A USB flash drive or a hard disc is one example of an external storage device. If you misplace the device's keycode or it malfunctions, you may never be able to retrieve your bitcoin. If you are locked out of your hot wallet, custodians can assist you in getting back into your account.

Buying Cryptocurrency in Other Ways

At the moment, purchasing cryptocurrency seems like a good investment idea, but it comes with a lot of volatility and danger. Here are a few alternatives to using an exchange or a broker to invest in Bitcoin or other cryptocurrencies:

Anticipate the Crypto Exchange-Traded Funds (ETFs)

Exchange-traded funds (ETFs) are a popular investment vehicle (ETFs), which provide you access to hundreds of different assets at once. Because of this, they are less hazardous than investing in individual assets and offer rapid diversification.

Many people are eager for bitcoin ETFs, which enable investors to invest in many cryptocurrencies at once. There are currently no cryptocurrency ETFs accessible to the general public, but this might change soon. Kryptcoin, VanEck, and WisdomTree have applied for three cryptocurrencies ETFs to be reviewed by the US Securities and Exchange Commission (SEC) as of June 2021.

Invest in Companies Connected to Cryptocurrency

To get a taste of the cryptocurrency market, you may want to explore investing in firms that utilize or own cryptocurrency and the blockchain that supports it. Governed oversight is in place. As an example of a publicly listed corporation in which to invest, consider

Nvidia (NVDA)

Mining cryptocurrencies relies on graphics processing units (GPUs), which this technological business manufactures and sells.

PayPal (PYPL)

In addition to purchasing goods and services online or sending money to loved ones, this payment network just included the ability to buy and sell various cryptocurrencies using PayPal and Venmo accounts.

Square (SQ)

People may now purchase, trade, and store cryptocurrencies with Square's Cash App. More than $220 million has been spent by a small-business payment service provider since October 2020 on Bitcoin purchases. The company revealed in February 2021 that Bitcoin accounted for almost 5% of its total cash on hand.

It's essential to consider your long-term financial objectives and present financial condition before investing in cryptocurrencies or cryptocurrency-related firms. One tweet may send the price of cryptocurrency plunging, making it a hazardous investment. As a result, funding should be approached with prudence and caution.

Crypto wallets

Using a wallet is the most secure method of storing your Bitcoin. Hosted wallets, non-custodial wallets, and hardware wallets are the most common forms of crypto wallets. The appropriate cryptocurrency for you will depend on your goals and desired level of security.

Hosted Wallets

Hosted wallets are the most popular and easy-to-use crypto wallets. It's termed "hosted" because a third party manages your crypto assets on your behalf, just as a bank does with your cash. On Coinbase, for example, your cryptocurrency is stored in a hosted wallet. If you've ever heard of somebody "dropping their keys" or "missing their USB wallet," you don't have to worry about that with a hosted wallet.

Keeping your cryptocurrency in an online wallet means you won't lose it if you misplace your password. A downside to using a hosted wallet is that you can't use all of the features of crypto. When it comes to hosted wallets, though, this may alter.

Hosted wallets: How to get started

Pick a reliable platform.

You must focus on three things: security, usability, and adherence to legal and financial mandates.

Open an account.

Choose a strong password and enter your personal information. Using two-step verification provides an additional degree of security (2FA).

Purchase cryptocurrencies or make a transfer of them.

It is possible to acquire cryptocurrency using a bank account or credit card on most crypto platforms and exchanges. Hosted wallets may be used to store any cryptocurrency that you currently hold.

Self-custody wallets

An independent wallet like Coinbase Wallet or MetaMask gives you complete control over your coins. Non-custodial wallets don't depend on a third party to protect your coin. While they supply the software to store your crypto, you are alone responsible for remembering and protecting your password. You can't access your crypto if you lose or forget your password (also called a "private key" or "seed phrase"). Anyone with your private key may access your assets.

A non-custodial wallet You can access complex crypto activities like yield farming, staking, lending, borrowing, and more. A hosted wallet is the simplest way for buying, selling, sending, and receiving bitcoin.

Creating a non-custodial wallet:

Get a wallet app

Like Coinbase Wallet and Meta Mask.

Open an account

Unlike a hosted wallet, a non-custodial wallet requires no personal information. Not even an email.

Note your secret key

It's a 12-word sentence. Please keep it safe. You can't access your crypto if you lose or forget this 12-word phrase.

Wallet crypto transfer

Buying crypto using fiat currency (such as dollars or euros) isn't always available, so you'll need to move crypto into your non-custodial wallet from somewhere. Customers of Coinbase may choose between a hosted and self-custody wallet. The Coinbase app is a hosted wallet. You may also use the Coinbase Wallet standalone app to benefit from a non-custodial wallet. It's simple to acquire crypto using regular cash and engage in sophisticated crypto activities for our consumers. Ether wallet setup is free.

Hardware wallets

Hardware wallets, which are more complicated and expensive, offer certain advantages, like the ability to keep your cryptocurrency safe even if your computer is compromised. Using a hardware wallet, the private keys to your cryptocurrency are saved on a device the size of a thumb drive. As a result, these devices are more challenging to use than software wallets, and they may cost as much as $100 to purchase.
Hardware wallet setup instructions:

Buy the hardware

It's hard to go wrong with either Ledger or Trezor.

Activate the software

Wallets may be set up with different software for each brand. Create your wallet by downloading the software from the company's website and following the instructions.

Transfer crypto to your wallet

To acquire crypto using conventional currencies (US dollars or euros), you'll need to transfer crypto into your hardware wallet, just like you would with a non-custodial wallet.
Cryptocurrency may be stored in various places, much like cash (in a bank account, a safe, or even beneath the mattress). When it comes to cryptocurrency, the choice is yours. You may use a hosted wallet to make things easy, or you can use a non-custodial wallet to have complete control over your crypto, or you can use a hardware wallet to be extra cautious.

Chapter 4: Crypto Portfolio and Market Capitalization

Cryptocurrencies are no different from regular investments when managing your portfolio. You may significantly lower your investment risk with the right profile and approach. Investing in several cryptocurrencies is all that is required to get started. Both sides of the debate are good and bad aspects when diversifying your portfolio. On the other hand, diversification is widely acknowledged as advantageous in moderation. Investing in various cryptocurrencies (including stablecoins) and regularly rebalancing your portfolio will help decrease your risk exposure. Using a third-party portfolio tracker or manually recording your transactions on a spreadsheet might help you better manage your portfolio. It is possible to connect specific trackers to your wallets and bitcoin exchanges, making the procedure simpler. When you buy your first cryptocurrency (BTC, ETH, etc.), you're on your way to becoming a crypto investor. The more prominent cryptocurrencies are preferred by confident investors, while others prefer to explore with altcoins. But how do we go about it? A well-balanced crypto portfolio is more likely to succeed if you consider your asset allocation carefully and do so frequently. There are several methods to do this, depending on your risk tolerance. It's not difficult to keep your portfolio under check, and the benefits may be substantial.

Crypto Portfolio

A **crypto portfolio** is a collection of crypto held by an investor or trader in the cryptocurrency world. Altcoins and other crypto-related financial instruments are standard components of portfolios. Like a regular investment portfolio, except that you're only investing in one asset type. If you want to check up on your cryptocurrency investments, you may do it manually using a spreadsheet or using specialist tools and software. A decent portfolio tracker is useful. Day traders and other short-term traders must use trackers, but long-term investors and HODLers may also benefit.

A **cryptocurrency portfolio** keeps track of your various digital currency holdings. It gives you the ability to keep tabs on each coin's progress and run multiple analyses on that data. Cryptocurrency exchanges offer many portfolio management systems real-time data feeds and price updates. They may notify you of significant market developments. While Bitcoin remains the most popular digital money, it should not be your only cryptocurrency investment. It's not uncommon for investors to invest in various cryptocurrencies to mitigate risk. But how can you pick which of the almost 3,000 cryptocurrencies to invest in? The ultimate objective is to have a diverse collection of cryptocurrencies.

According to cryptocurrency specialists, you should only invest in digital currencies you fully understand and have done significant research on. That is good advice. You do the same thing with traditional assets like stocks and bonds. In the words of Benjamin Franklin: "The highest return on an investment is knowledge."

Diversified and Concentrated Portfolio

There are both advantages and disadvantages to diversifying your investment portfolio. The consensus is that you need to have a well-diversified cryptocurrency portfolio. As we've previously established, a well-diversified portfolio lowers an investment's total risk and volatility. Gains may counterbalance losses, allowing you to maintain your position. With each coin in your collection, you have additional options to generate money. With correct asset allocation and diversification, you have a better chance of making money in the long term.

In order to achieve more profits, most traders and investors want to outperform the market. However, the closer your portfolio tracks the broader market, the more diversified it is. The average return from a well-diversified portfolio is higher than the average return from a concentrated one. Low-earning ones might offset High-earning assets. To correctly manage a diverse portfolio, you'll need to put in more time and effort. To make wise investments, you must know what you're getting into. Having a vast portfolio reduces one's ability to comprehend everything. You may need to utilize various wallets and exchanges to access your assets if they're spread across different blockchains. Whether or whether you choose to diversify is entirely up to you, but it's always a good idea.

Asset allocations and diversification

You should be conversant with asset allocation and diversification ideas while putting up an investment portfolio. Investing in various asset types is known as asset allocation (e.g., cryptocurrencies, stocks, bonds, precious metals, cash, etc.). In the context of investing, diversification refers to distributing your money across various investments or industries. There are several ways to vary your investments, such as by investing in a wide range of various sectors. Both of these methods will lower your total exposure to danger. Cryptocurrencies may be considered a single asset class from a technical perspective. The advantage of diversification in a cryptocurrency portfolio is that it allows you to own various assets with varying objectives and use cases. According to this example: 40 percent Bitcoin, 30 percent Stablecoin and 15 percent NFT.

Types of Cryptocurrencies in your Portfolio

The new asset class of cryptocurrencies offers more significant profits and more significant risks. They are gaining traction throughout the globe and should be included in any future secure portfolio that you put up. When you first join, you may allocate up to 2% of your portfolio to crypto, and you can gradually grow that percentage over time. Fixed deposits, gold, real estate, and even free cash may all be used to offset these risks. It would be best if you conceived of as your crypto capital is the money you can afford to lose. When market volatility hits you hard on the downside, you won't be harmed as much since you've minimized your exposure to the risky asset.

Payment coins

New currencies that deal solely with payments are rare to come by these days. Historically, however, most cryptocurrency initiatives have been mechanisms for exchanging value. Ripple, Bitcoin Cash (BCH), and Litecoin (LTC) are a few additional examples of decentralized digital currencies worth noting. Before Ethereum and smart contracts, these coins were the initial generation of cryptocurrencies.

Stablecoins

Some stablecoins seek to mimic the value of tangible assets, such as gold and silver. BUSD, for example, uses a 1:1 reserve ratio to tie the U.S. dollar to the BUSD. Unlike PAX, which is based on the price of a single troy ounce of fine gold, PAX Gold (PAXG) employs a different methodology entirely. Stablecoins don't always bring in big profits, but they keep their value steady. Having a stable asset in your portfolio might be helpful in the turbulent cryptocurrency market. A drop in the crypto market shouldn't harm a stable coin if it is pegged to anything other than the crypto ecosystem. Using a dollar-backed stable coin like BUSD, you can quickly transfer tokens out of a coin or project to protect your profits. Transacting with money requires more time and effort than doing so in exchange for a stable coin.

Security Tokens

A security token, like conventional securities, may stand for a variety of things. Equity in a firm or a bond from a project might be a form of compensation. Essentially, guarantees have been digitized and placed on the blockchain, which means that the same set of rules governs them. Due to this, security tokens are subject to the authority of local authorities and must go through a legal procedure before issue.

Utility Tokens

If you want to get into a service or product, you'll need some kind of token. BNB and ETH, for example, are utility tokens. You may use them to pay transaction fees while using decentralized apps, among other things (DApps). Several projects create their utility tokens to raise money via a coin offering. The token's value should presumably be linked to the value of its usefulness.

Governance Tokens

Having a governance token enables you to vote on a project and even a portion of the profits generated by that project. PancakeSwap, Uniswap, and SushiSwap are decentralized finance (Defi) systems. When a project succeeds, so does the value of a governance token, much like utility tokens.

Crypto Market Capitalization

An individual **cryptocurrency's market capitalization** represents the entire worth of all of its circulating units. The crypto market capitalization is calculated by multiplying the price of the cryptocurrency by the number of coins in circulation instead of the stock market capitalization, which is calculated by multiplying the share price by the outstanding shares.

There are over 18 billion Bitcoins in existence, and their market value is calculated by multiplying the current price of Bitcoin by that amount. Market capitalization changes with Bitcoin's price, which is the case regularly. Bitcoin's price has fluctuated between $45,000 to $55,000 in the last several weeks, resulting in a significant shift in the cryptocurrency's market capitalization:

- Eight hundred and forty-six billion dollars
- $50,000 multiplied by 18,8 million is $940 billion.
- $55,000 divided by 18.8 million is $1.034 trillion.

Ethereum's market capitalization is compared to Bitcoin's in the following table: Ethereum has a market value of $351 billion, with a price of $3,000 per coin and an overall supply of about 117 million coins in circulation worldwide. Ethereum's market valuation is higher even though many more coins are in circulation.

Crypto Weighted Market Cap Strategy

A weighted market cap strategy entails investing a certain percentage of your money into each asset class based on market capitalization. Since Bitcoin and Ethereum each have different rates of the entire market capitalization, you'd get 71% for Bitcoin and 29% for Ethereum when dividing the total by the percentages held by each cryptocurrency.

You can figure out how much to invest in the two main cryptocurrencies, Bitcoin and Ethereum: On the Ethereum side, you'd support around $29. If you want to invest a certain percentage of your overall investment in each coin, divide the total by the market capitalization of each coin. If nothing else, this assures you're investing lesser amounts into other cryptos and more significant amounts into Bitcoin and Ethereum, both of which are secure. Despite what the experts say, the same idea can be applied to any asset you choose to include in your portfolio, even if it's not Bitcoin.

Furthermore, it's essential to keep in mind that the market capitalization of cryptocurrencies fluctuates continuously. Because of this volatility and the possibility of a market collapse, experts advise investors to restrict their investments to a minimum and only invest what they are willing to lose.

Crypto Market Cap for Investors

You may classify a firm into one of three investing categories: small, mid, or large-cap based on its market value. There are various reasons why an investor would decide to split their investment into multiple categories; therefore, understanding the market cap is critical. As measured by its market cap, maybe the valuation is a good indicator of how hazardous it is to invest in it. Investing in large-cap companies might be less risky, but the returns are longer to materialize.

However, Bitcoin is a relatively new phenomenon. It's so fresh that these kinds of categories have yet to be established. Using market cap in making investment choices is less necessary now that experts recommend sticking to Bitcoin and Ethereum and not allowing crypto to account for more than 5% of your whole portfolio. To better understand a token's potential, you may want to know its market cap, but it shouldn't play a significant role in your investment selections as it does on the stock market. With crypto, "It's crucial to know that it's different from the stock market," explains Jully Alma-Taveras, the personal finance expert behind "'Investing Latina'" on Instagram. This is an entirely new world. While market capitalization has a more restricted use with crypto trading, there is one method that might influence the way you invest in Bitcoin and Ethereum.

Market Cap Ratio

You can make better investing selections by comparing one cryptocurrency's market cap to another's. The market capitalization of cryptocurrencies may be divided into three categories:

- More than $10 billion worth of **large-cap cryptocurrencies**, including Bitcoin and Ethereum. As a result, investors see them as low-risk investments since they have a proven track record of growth and can survive a more significant number of individuals selling without significantly affecting the price.
- The market capitalization of **mid-cap cryptocurrencies** ranges from $1 billion to $10 billion, and they are often thought to have more upside potential and more significant risk than large-cap cryptocurrencies.
- Market mood may have a tremendous impact on **small-cap cryptocurrencies**, which have a market capitalization of less than $1 billion.

For comparison purposes, the market capitalization may be informative. Still, it's important to consider other factors such as market trends, a cryptocurrency's stability, and your financial status before making an investing decision.

Large Cap

If a cryptocurrency's market capitalization is more than $10 billion, it is considered a "large-cap." According to that estimation, there are now just four large-cap currencies in the market. Only Bitcoin, Ethereum, USDT (stable coin), and XRP are available in this writing. It's safe to say that these cryptocurrencies have a long track record of reliability and security, making them critical participants in the market.

Mid Cap

The market capitalization of mid-cap coins and tokens ranges from USD 1 billion to USD 10 billion. Already established, these initiatives are growing and may see considerable expansion shortly. Chain Link, Cardano, Litecoin, Tezos, Monero, and Binance Coin is among the most popular currencies and tokens in this category.

Small-Cap

These initiatives lack experience and funding compared to the most successful ones. Their age and size put them in greater danger than smaller coins. Moreover, $100 million in market value, but less than $1 billion, is considered a small-cap. However, when you do your research and check at low-cap currencies carefully, you may uncover one that has enormous growth potential.

High Liquidity, Low Volatility, and Low Risk Characterize Large-Cap Stocks

Large-cap cryptocurrencies are the least dangerous of the three. You won't see big returns in a short period by investing in significant companies, but you will see steady growth over time. Liquidity is strong for coins with significant market capitalization. It signifies that these currencies can be found on most cryptocurrency exchanges and have a large volume of activity. Investors may quickly enter and exit a market with a high level of liquidity. A multiple purchase or sell order may be placed, and the order will be completed instantly. Larger companies are less volatile, making it more challenging to influence the price in any way. In spite of this, they're still more volatile than more established investments, such as equities.

Mid-Caps: Medium Risk, Decent Liquidity, and Enormous Growth Potential

The risk and volatility of mid-cap cryptos are greater than those of large-cap cryptos. They aren't as well-known as the big ones. Many mid-cap currencies have yet to achieve their full potential since their usefulness is still expanding. In comparison to big-cap currencies, they thus have more significant growth potential. Mid-cap cryptocurrencies, on the whole, tend to do well over the long term, making them an excellent diversification tool. Even yet, keep in mind that not every coin has the potential to become a significant cap.

Small Caps: - High Risk, Volatile, and Lacking Liquidity

A cryptocurrency's volatility is a significant determinant of risk. Since smaller market caps tend to be more volatile than larger ones, a coin's price may fluctuate more often. Put another way, small market size companies are more vulnerable to price changes. An enormous purchase or sell order has the power to change the price quickly. Your investment in this instrument is hazardous because of the rapid increase and price fall. As a result, small-cap stocks are more susceptible to market sentiment. A single favorable or bad media report may easily make or destroy a coin since these coins are generally new and have little history.

Final Thoughts

Investing in cryptocurrencies isn't just about choosing coins based on their market capitalization. A cryptocurrency's market capitalization is a good indicator of its popularity and market domination. Not all metrics are created equal, though. In addition to the project's core team, fundamentals, technical, and value proposition, you should consider these additional aspects while making your cryptocurrency selection.

Then there is the number of coins and tokens, which significantly impacts the market valuation. To improve their position in the CMC rankings, the majority of centralized projects may burn coins and change the parameters of the currency supply. Before purchasing a cryptocurrency, an investor should do extensive due diligence on the project. Check out the project's history. ' The daily traded volume of most mid-and small-cap currencies is heavily controlled, so keep an eye on it as well. Do not be fooled by currency promotions that promise the moon in YouTube videos or Twitter profiles. Because this is a speculative asset class, you should only invest at your own risk and make your own investment choices.

Chapter 5: Most Important Crypto Coins

Complex cryptography is used to create and handle digital currencies and their transactions over distributed networks, thus the term "crypto" in cryptocurrency. Decentralization is a frequent "crypto" trait, and cryptocurrencies are often produced as code by teams that include methods for issuance (usually, but not always, via a mining process) and other regulations. The core component of the cryptocurrency sector is that it is supposed to be free of government manipulation and control; however, this has come under scrutiny as the industry has risen in popularity. Altcoins, and even shitcoins, are a collective term for Bitcoin-inspired cryptocurrencies that have attempted to promote themselves as better or more advanced versions of Bitcoin. Even if they may boast capabilities that Bitcoin doesn't, Altcoins have yet to reach the degree of security achieved by Bitcoin's networks.

But first, a disclaimer: A list like this will never be complete. There are over 8,000 decentralized cryptocurrencies in regulation as of January 2022, which is one cause for this. 1 These cryptos, despite their lack of notoriety or trading volume, have a strong following and support among their supporters and investors. Furthermore, the area of cryptocurrencies is constantly evolving, and the next significant digital token might be created as soon as today. Analysts use various methods to assess tokens other than Bitcoin, even though it is often regarded as a pioneer in the realm of cryptocurrencies. Analysts, for example, tend to place a lot of emphasis on the relative market capitalization of different cryptocurrencies. This has been taken into account. However, a digital token might also be provided for other reasons.

Bitcoin

A decentralized digital currency known as Bitcoin may be purchased, sold, and exchanged without the need for a bank or other middleman. According to Bitcoin's initial developer Satoshi Nakamoto, a "cryptographic evidence instead of faith" payment method was needed.

BTC transactions are recorded in the public database that is open to the world, making them impossible to reverse or spoof. That's the goal: There is no central authority or issuing organization to support Bitcoins, which is a crucial characteristic of the currency's decentralized structure. Anton Mozgovoy is the co-founder and chief executive officer of the digital financial services business Holyhead and believes that the only reason anything has a monetary value is that we as a society have determined that it does. Bitcoin's value has increased considerably since first made public in 2009. Today, a single Bitcoin costs more than $62,000, even though it was formerly valued at less than $150 per coin. For this reason, many believe that its price will continue to rise as more major investment firms start treating it as a kind of virtual gold as a hedge against market volatility and inflation.

Why Purchase Bitcoin?

Cryptocurrency exchanges are the most common method of purchasing Bitcoin. As with creating a brokerage or bank account for buying, selling, and holding cryptocurrencies, you'll need to authenticate your identity and offer some form of money source to create a cryptocurrency exchange account. Coinbase, Kraken, and Gemini are all well-known exchanges. Online brokers like Robinhood allow you to acquire Bitcoin. A Bitcoin wallet is required regardless of where your Bitcoin is purchased. This is either a hot or a cold wallet depending on the temperature. It is possible to store cryptocurrency in a hot wallet (also known as an online wallet) hosted by an exchange or service provider in the cloud. Exodus, Electrum, and Mycelium are just a few of the many online wallet service providers. A mobile wallet is a device used to store Bitcoin offline and is not linked to the web.

Due to its near-synonymous status with cryptocurrency, Bitcoin can be purchased on practically any crypto exchange, whether you're using fiat money or another crypto asset. BTC trading is offered in several major markets, including:

- Binance
- OKEx
- Coinbase Pro
- Kraken
- Huobi Global
- Bitfinex

Alexandria, CoinMarketCap's educational site, is a great place to start learning about purchasing Bitcoin and other cryptocurrencies if you're new to the space.

The following are a few things to keep in mind while purchasing Bitcoin: You may be able to acquire fractions of Bitcoin from specific retailers, despite the high cost of Bitcoin. Bitcoin purchases mustn't be immediate as many other equities transactions seem to be. Miners must verify all Bitcoin transactions before they appear in your account, which may take anywhere from 10-20 minutes.

Investing Bitcoin

Investing in Bitcoin is similar to holding stock. Bitcoin IRAs, a new kind of retirement account, make it possible to do so now. People invest in different ways: some purchase and keep for the long term; others buy and hope to sell at a profit when the price rises; still others wager that the price will fall. The price of Bitcoin has fluctuated dramatically throughout the years, dropping as low as $5,165 in 2020 and as high as $28,990 in the same year.

However, "Bitcoin is an asset that appears like it will be gaining in value quite fast for some time," adds Marquez; in certain regions, people may use Bitcoin to pay for items. "So why would you sell something that will be valued so much more in a year than it is now??" The vast majority of those who retain it do so for the long haul. A Bitcoin mutual fund is also available to the general public, but only to accredited investors that earn at least $200,000 or have net worths of at least $1 million, which is presently the case with the Grayscale Bitcoin Trust (GBTC). To put it another way, the vast majority of Americans cannot afford it. However, Bitcoin diversification is becoming more accessible in Canada. Purpose Bitcoin ETF (BTCC) and Evolve Bitcoin ETF (EBIT) were authorized by the Ontario Securities Commission in February 2021 as the world's first Bitcoin ETFs. Investors in the United States who are hoping to get exposure to the technology behind cryptocurrencies may explore blockchain ETFs. Although crypto-based funds may help diversify cryptocurrency holdings and reduce risk significantly, they nevertheless do so at a considerably higher cost and with far more trouble than traditional index funds. Index-based mutual and exchange-traded funds may be a good choice for investors who want to build wealth over time (ETFs).

Bitcoin in Circulation

According to Bitcoin's software, there will never be more than 21,000,000 coins in circulation at any one time. The procedure known as "mining" is used to produce new coins. When transactions are sent over the network, miners pick them up and bundle them into blocks safeguarded by complicated cryptographic computations. For each block that is successfully added to the blockchain, the miners are rewarded for using their computer resources. With every 210,000 additional blocks mined — a process that takes the network around four years — the payout for mining, a bitcoin is half to only 25 bitcoins. There will be just 6.25 bitcoins in the block reward in 2020.

Premined Bitcoin does not indicate that the creators of Bitcoin had any coins mined and distributed before the public release of Bitcoin. Competition amongst miners was relatively low in the early years of BTC's existence, enabling early network players to amass large quantities of coins via frequent mining: Satoshi Nakamoto alone is estimated to control a million BTC moreover. If the current hash rate and the price of Bitcoin are favorable, mining Bitcoins may be a lucrative endeavor for miners. We examine how long it takes to mine one Bitcoin on CoinMarketCap, although mining Bitcoins is complicated. After the 2020 halving, the Bitcoin mining reward will be limited to 6.25 BTC, or $299,200 at today's pricing, by the middle of September 2021.

Ethereum

Ethereum is a decentralized and open-source blockchain. Ether (ETH) is the platform's native currency. The market capitalization of Ether is second only to that of Bitcoin. Gavin Wood, Charles Hoskinson, Anthony Di Iorio, and Joseph Lubin were Ethereum's co-founders. It's a platform that anybody can use to build and run permanent, decentralized apps that other users can interact with. There is no need for traditional financial intermediaries like brokerages, exchanges, or banks to offer a wide range of financial services in Defi apps, such as enabling cryptocurrency consumers to lend on their stocks or lend them out for interest. It is also viable to use Ethereum to create and trade non-transferable tokens (NFTs) linked to virtual pieces of art or other actual commodities and marketed as unique digital property. On top of Ethereum's blockchain, numerous other cryptocurrencies use ERC-20 tokens and have raised money via ICOs on Ethereum.

Ethereum 2.0, a set of enhancements that involves a switch to proof of stake and attempts to boost transaction throughput via sharding, has begun implementation.

Performance in 2020

Ethereum's revival was set for 2020. So even if 2020 didn't hit a new all-time high, its foundation should allow for a further price increase. More than $90 billion worth of total value was trapped in Ethereum or ERC20 tokens based on Ethereum since DeFi's first explosion. Ethereum-based Defi and NFTs are in great demand, driving up the price of ETH as a way to pay for the exorbitantly high gas costs. Scalability and investment success are two critical goals for the next Ethereum 2.0 version implemented in stages. ETH has already reached an all-time high of $2,000 per ETH owing to exceptional demand to pay for gas expenses in 2021, positive for Ethereum. Ethereum's ecosystem has developed to such a size that it's unlikely to be overtaken by newcomers. The total value locked in Ethereum has surpassed $90 billion, and the demand for the cryptocurrency is only going to increase, and the supply will decrease as that continues. Most of the Ethereum in circulation is now held in smart contracts, with a large portion of it held at Ethereum 2.0's staking address. EIP 1559, a new upgrade, is expected to significantly influence the supply of Ethereum, making ETH increasingly rare over time. Ethereum may be a better investment than even Bitcoin because of all of these considerations, as well as Wall Street's conviction that Ethereum is here to stay. However, there is still the possibility that this bullish currency has run out of steam after such a significant increase in 2020 and 2021. The remainder of the year is up in the air.

Ethereum Investing

By purchasing Ethereum, you are making a long-term bet on the future of money. The smart contract platform has already started substituting shares and bonds with tokens connected to smart contracts in some corporate operations, displacing Wall Street's outdated, antiquated backend. Since Ethereum is a platform for developers to create and innovate on, its potential is maybe even more incredible than Bitcoin's. An excellent example of this is the current Defi craze. In finance, there is always a new and exciting initiative or addition that sets the sector on a new path. New buzzwords like "yield farming" and "liquidity pooling" have been coined as a result. Scams and projects with no real-world use are common, but there are also plenty of gems to be found. Traditional finance is being disrupted by promising Defi initiatives that enable permissionless lending and borrowing. Non-fungible tokens, or the NFT market, play a vital role in the evolution of the Ethereum price since most NFTs are developed using a different standard for Ethereum smart contracts. Ethereum-based blockchains, such as Defi, need those transactions to be paid for using ETH as gas.

Regardless of what these initiatives become or how they evolve, Ethereum and its investors will reap the benefits. Ethereum has recently outperformed Bitcoin and practically all other cryptocurrencies because of the Defi craze, making it an excellent investment for 2021. Even though Ethereum has already achieved a new all-time high, Ethereum's current upswing may be just getting started, which means that now is the best moment to buy in the cryptocurrency.

Crypto to invest in 2022

On Wednesday, the most popular cryptocurrencies sank sharply as a broad Nasdaq sell-off resumed for the third day in a row. Investors were scared away from riskier assets such as cryptocurrency when the Federal Reserve promised eight interest rate increases over three years, putting a damper on the flames of the financial crisis.
Avalanche (CRYPTO: AVAX), Terra (CRYPTO: LUNA), Solana (CRYPTO: SOL, CRYPTO: LUNA, and CRYPTO: SOL) were all down more than ten percent in the last 24 hours, according to statistics from CoinGecko.com when markets reopened on Thursday.

Solana

During the Asian-Pacific trading session on Tuesday, Solana's token was trading at $105.6 per token, a decrease of over 50 percent since January. Since January 28, the digital asset has gained 20 percent and has maintained a solid resistance-turned-support line of $86.6. There is a resistance trendline in SOL's recent bullish efforts, though. Solana might rise to at least $128.0 if it breaks through the support level. Solana-based coins were added to Coinbase, the biggest cryptocurrency exchange in the United States. Coinbase says the FIDA/ORCA pair will begin trading on February 1 at 9 a.m. Pacific Time.

Terra

It's still too early to predict a complete return to November's all-time highs after the January freefall. Terra's governance token, LUNA, has risen 15% in the last two days, suggesting a possible retest of the previous support level. TVL has a market capitalization of $13.7 billion as of the first trading day of February. While other Defi systems saw a significant drop in TVL, Terra's was not as affected. Since 2021, its market share has risen from 0.46 percent in March 2021 to a solid 7 percent in February 2022. With Terra's recent daily increase, Terra also surpassed Binance Smart Chain (BSC) in terms of market cap and moved silver to the level of gold held by Ethereum (ETH).

Avalanche

With a $17 billion market worth, Avalanche, another Ethereum killer, fell over 40% in January. Despite this, the digital asset has been steadily rising since January 22. Like SOL and LUNA, it is premature to expect a complete recovery before the end of the year. The token's setup might fuel a bullish bias.

A bullish reversal pattern is known as the "Falling Wedge," representing a bullish setup. AVAX might break the resistance trendline and reach the support bar at $80.0 to $85.0 by following the formation.

Crypto Staking

Many cryptocurrency exchanges have implemented incentive schemes to assist individuals in gaining more value out of their digital assets, even though these marketplaces have typically concentrated on offering a location to purchase and trade digital assets. In terms of their details, each of these initiatives is unique. "Staking" your cryptocurrency, or using it to help verify transactions on the blockchain network, might earn you money in some instances. Others allow users to earn income on their assets by storing them on a platform via lending programs. Below, you'll find information on each platform's reward scheme. NerdWallet-reviewed exchanges that will enable consumers to utilize their bitcoins to earn rewards are included in this list.

It's important to think about the rates at which rewards may be earned, how frequently they're given out, how simple it is to remove your holdings from the program, and how many qualifying cryptocurrencies there are when selecting an exchange for staking or rewards. In addition, we looked at important aspects of any exchange service, such as the quality of the website and the ratings of mobile apps.

Nexo Wallet

Nexo is an ERC20 security token that pays interest and is certified by the corporate marketplaces to be SEC-compliant. Developed by Credissmo, a Fintech business based in Europe, Nexo is a cryptocurrency-backed lending system. Instant cash in EUR or USD may be received by depositing the supported digital currencies into a Nexo wallet. Nexo was first given through airdrop before being made available for sale as a token. Clients may now deposit their NEXO dividend tokens into their Nexo wallets as of June 4th, 2018, making this a significant step toward creating the industry's first credit product of institution-grade.

Celsius Wallet

Although Celsius isn't regulated like a traditional bank, it functions. Weekly interest payments are made to those who deposit Bitcoin, Ethereum, or Tether. On the other hand, Celsius pays interest rates that are tens or hundreds of times greater than those offered by regular banks. To put it another way, it has doubled its assets to $25 billion in the past year. When Mashinsky informs his Celsius users that they can aid the poor and fight back against greedy banks via Celsius, they give him a standing ovation since he has helped them earn enough money to repay loans or even leave their employment. It is worth noting that Canadian pension fund Caisse de Dépôt and Placement du Québec invested another $750 million in Celsius last year. A $3 billion value of the investment round made Mashinsky a multi-billionaire.

Chapter 6: The future of Crypto

In the future, we may guess about what value bitcoin may have for investors (and many wills), but the truth is that it is still a very new and speculative investment, and there isn't much history on which to make forecasts. Nothing an expert says or believes will change that no one knows for sure. So, it's crucial to stick to more traditional assets for long-term wealth creation rather than risking all you have. Would you be okay when the developed countries prohibit cryptocurrency and lose its value? Life water Wealth Management's CFP Frederick Stanfield recently spoke to Next Advisor on diversifying one's portfolio. Don't put your crypto investments ahead of anything else, including retirement savings or paying off high-interest debt. Instead, keep your assets modest.

Cryptocurrencies such as Bitcoin and others. Cryptocurrencies like Bitcoin and Ethereum are essentially trustless since they are not tied to any government or other institution. Because it is not tied to a single government, cryptocurrency advocates argue that it is better than traditional fiat currencies. Grundfest points out that this isn't correct, regardless of how you feel about it. In reality, cryptocurrencies aren't entirely trustworthy. For the time being, they are still heavily dependent on the backbone of cryptocurrencies like Bitcoin, most of it situated inside the Chinese government. It is theoretically possible for China's government to make significant changes to cryptocurrencies by forcing its will on the data miners who power them.

Many of the oddest news in 2021 was about cryptocurrency. It was said that digital currencies might revolutionize the globe and empower individuals who don't have bank accounts. Cryptocurrency's environmental impact and use in online crime were cited as points of contention by its detractors. It will be challenging to bridge the abyss between these two points of view. There is a lot of buzz in the bitcoin market because of all the weird dog and outer-space emoji jokes. On the same business, venture capitalists and individual enthusiasts have invested an incredible amount of money in actual technological advancements that might fundamentally transform the way we interact with money. We may not receive what we anticipate from new technology, as is so frequently the case.

Cryptocurrency to gain more traction in the mainstream.

Cryptocurrency is being examined by some of the world's largest corporations. This year, everyone from hedge fund managers to Starbucks CEOs makes decisions that might significantly influence how we utilize digital money. Cryptocurrency is often associated with Elon Musk's tweets, overnight billionaires, pricey digital art, and hacks when it appears in the news headlines. However, the more fundamental, long-term developments are typically overlooked in favor of the daily crypto-hype machine. Denelle Dixon, CEO of Stellar Development Foundation, stated, "I think we're going to see a lot more attention on usefulness." "An increased emphasis on use cases that provide actual value will replace a narrow concentration on just a few popular use cases. There will also be increasing debate over financial inclusion."

Libra: It's not all that it seems to be

Facebook's foray into the cryptocurrency realm, Libra, has been heralded as the panacea to a slew of financial ills by some. Additionally, the platform was meant to simplify international payments and remove transaction fees. Professor Grundfest admits that the objective is noble, but he thinks the technique is faulty. He doesn't believe that launching a new cryptocurrency is the best way to reduce payment transactions, and he doesn't support Facebook's efforts to avoid altogether established banking institutions.

A preferable strategy for Facebook would have been to develop a significant financial institution for its users, according to Professor Grundfest. Better use of firm resources would have been to establish banking systems tailored to the needs of each country or area, meet regulatory requirements, and reduce expenses. To develop a global network, all that is needed is to connect each existing one and build public confidence.

Cryptocurrency: Stable Coin the Future

Like the gold standard, stable coins have become more popular to underpin bitcoin with real-world assets. There are a wide variety of investments that may be used as collateral. Grundfest has a few concerns with this strategy. For starters, it re-creates an existing system. Because it's difficult to audit and monitor, it might make it simpler for criminals to perpetrate fraud than conventional currencies.

On the last slide of his presentation, Professor Grundfest discussed some of the cryptocurrency's most robust use cases. Investors in nations with weak currencies, for example, may benefit more from putting their money in Bitcoin than in local equities or bonds. The future of cryptocurrency is still very much up in the air. On the other hand, critics perceive nothing but the danger in the idea of a new product or service. Although Professor Grundfest remains skeptical, he acknowledges that bitcoin can be used in certain situations.

Bitcoin and other cryptocurrencies have become a phenomenon in the media because of their volatility. In the blink of an eye, you may become a multimillionaire or lose all you've worked for. But if you attempt to purchase a coffee with bitcoin, things might become a little tricky quickly.

Stable coins are a solution to this problem. There's less volatility in this subgroup of cryptocurrency since it is linked to an asset. To make cryptocurrencies more accessible, stable coins might play an essential role in making it easier to perform our regular transactions.

"Stable coins, both as a payment method and as a digital currency pegged to the dollar, are something to keep an eye on. Stable coins have the potential to speed up the transfer of assets. This value is significant for businesses that need the rapid and efficient transfer of digital assets and cash. In 2021, cross-border payments, assistance relief, and prompt settlement payments will all experience an increase in popularity, "In an email, Circle vice president of product Rachel Mayer said.

Crypto Market Prediction for Future

Throughout 2021, cryptocurrency investors were on high alert because of the new year. Since the beginning of the year, Bitcoin (CRYPTO: BTC) and Ethereum (CRYPTO: ETH) were up 309% and 459%, respectively. 2020's bullish market momentum carried over into robust gains in 2021, according to the latest data. As a result of the rise of Bitcoin and Ethereum, tens of thousands of altcoins had their first taste of popular success. However, the broad market trend has been slowly rising, albeit a bumpy ride. Cryptocurrency and its investors' long-term trajectory will be decided by the 2022 calendar, which will resolve specific critical concerns that have remained unanswered in past years.

In 2022 and beyond, it's hard to predict what will happen in the bitcoin industry. There are a lot more questions than there are answers. As the crypto market continues to change, you will be able to make smarter investment choices if you keep an eye on a few underlying trends. The following three specifics must be adhered to:

- Regulating in the United States as well as elsewhere.
- Cryptocurrency payments are gaining traction in the mainstream.
- Bitcoin ETFs and other digital currency ETFs are traded on exchanges.

A clear picture of the cryptocurrency industry's long-term prospects will emerge when these problems are addressed and remedied over time. A constant stream of incremental development has been made since Bitcoin's inception. Our understanding of what's going on will improve by the end of 2022.

Cryptocurrency: The Currency of The Future

By 2022, authorities throughout the globe might come up with a worldwide framework for regulating cryptocurrencies. Treasury Secretary Janet Yellen and Securities and Exchange Commission Chairman Gary Gensler have been brought together by the Biden administration to lead the cryptocurrency regulatory process. Yellen has been keeping tabs on this industry for years, but with a cautious eye. In 2018, Gensler was a visiting professor at MIT, where he taught courses on bitcoin, blockchains, and other cryptocurrencies.

There is genuine optimism that a functional system can be built for investors, consumers, cryptocurrency firms, and conventional institutions if well-informed individuals set the tone for future laws. Regulators who are well-versed in these matters will distinguish between, for example, the differences between a value storage system like Bitcoin and an advanced ledger with smart contracts like Ethereum.

Once the federal government has established a legal framework and taxation system, a considerable number of cryptocurrencies may reach the digital wallets of American residents. However, despite El Salvador accepting Bitcoin as legal cash in 2021, the United States is unlikely to follow suit soon. Soon, however, many merchants are expected to accept payment in digital currencies similar to cash, such as Bitcoin, Ripple's XRP, or Litecoin (CRYPTO: LTC). The growing popularity of cryptocurrency should prompt regulation and political action, and blockchain systems should gain from this as well.

In 2022 and beyond, these procedures will permeate the crypto economy. So even an unduly tight regulatory framework would be welcomed by investors who are fed up with today's incoherent monitoring.

Future hacks and ransoms

In 2021, cryptocurrency was used to finance ransomware payments of millions of dollars. This is because digital currencies have qualities that make them appealing to thieves. Once payment has been made, it's practically hard to reverse a payment; tracking and tracing them is very tough once payment has been made. Gurvais Grigg, a senior tech officer at Chainalysis, stated in an email that "we should anticipate seeing more criminals flocking to cryptocurrencies and services that promise to conceal illegal cash owing to the misperception of ultimate anonymity." When used for lawful purposes, Bitcoin is attractive to criminals because it is cross-border, fast, and liquid.

In 2022, Grigg and others predict that cryptocurrency-based decentralized finance would be a favorite target for hackers due to its small but growing business. A single authority or organization that doesn't control financing is called Defi or decentralized finance. People may directly connect to Defi items over a dispersed network rather than depending on a bank or credit card network. Defi is a fast-moving, high-tech business with a lot of promise, even if it's still in its infancy. Consequently, it has garnered interest and money, making it an ideal target for criminals.

According to Grigg, for both hacking and money laundering purposes, criminals are likely to investigate Defi. "These systems are ideal targets for experienced criminals who have made similar attacks previously, due to how new Defi is and the boom in use in developed economies."

Cryptocurrency regulations are on the rise

Legislators in Olympia recognize the significance of cryptocurrencies. The difficulty in grasping it is, nonetheless, evident. The "series of tubes" moment for crypto may be just around the corner, courtesy of an unprepared representative. Whether it comes to cryptocurrency, lawmakers in the United States have indicated an interest in a wide variety of issues, including whether stable coin producers should be deemed banks and when to tax cryptocurrency. It's a thorny subject. It will take some time to have the correct standards in place.

American citizens may have to wait to see a complete framework for crypto-focused legislation before further milestones are reached. However, normal bitcoin users and investors may gain while business leaders and political authorities collaborate while environmental and security issues are addressed. Because of this, we should expect even more radical changes as the bitcoin market matures. There's no doubt about it: Cryptocurrency will play a role in our future.

Crypto: What the Future Holds

The volatility and component of cryptocurrencies, particularly Bitcoin, has been well-documented throughout the years. Volatility in Bitcoin is mainly determined by the choices made by financial authorities in the United States regarding its use. When everything is said and done, it may be summed like this: Users of Bitcoin believe that by 2024, roughly 94% of the many Bitcoin varieties will be revealed.

According to Snapchat's original investor, Jeremy Liew, Bitcoin might reach a whopping $500,000 by 2030. Because it is decentralized, secure, and anonymous, this kind of cash is projected to expand in popularity dramatically. Cryptocurrencies like Bitcoin have a bright future since many tech-savvy people and businesses choose to use alternative encrypted currency forms. Miners used to make a lot of money when they added new blocks to the blockchain, but that is expected to go away soon. Even though cryptocurrency is only getting started, it is too early to predict whether or not the next big thing is money or what impact it will have in the future. Suppose a computer crashes and wipes all the information, including the crypto wallets. In that case, the loss of all crypto portfolios might be prevented in the future, thanks to technological improvements. Other advantages include a possible defense against hackers who may wipe away your whole bank account within seconds. As more companies embrace crypto as a payment method, its adoption has grown.

To jump into the technology revolution, several governments have begun developing their cryptocurrencies, and legislation has been issued in many countries to restrict the usage of these currencies, giving them greater credibility as a form of cash for businesses and people to utilize. It is expected that the use of crypto would increase due to more restrictions. The safety of a currency is an important consideration, and bitcoin meets this need admirably. Because it is open source and has never been hacked, blockchain proves to be very secure. If a company in the ecosystem has a weakness in its website and links to information that can be used to hack wallets, Bitcoin may be hacked. However, cryptocurrency is broadly safe and can be used for a long time like money in the future.

Conclusion

Cryptocurrency's future is bright because of its widespread popularity and acceptance. As crypto grows, a lot of stability and a store of value will be achieved. It may be used more broadly by businesses, the government, and individuals in their everyday lives. In the early phases of its development, cryptocurrency is still a bit of a mystery, and some people are still hesitant about it. Still, it is here to stay, has been adopted into our daily lives, and will soon be utilized by everyone.

www.ingramcontent.com/pod-product-compliance
Lightning Source LLC
LaVergne TN
LVHW082035050326
832904LV00005B/186